I
HEARD
GOD
TALKING
TO
ME

I HEARD GOD TALKING TO ME

~

William Edmondson and His Stone Carvings

ELIZABETH SPIRES

FRANCES FOSTER BOOKS

Farrar, Straus and Giroux ❧ New York

Farrar, Straus and Giroux
18 West 18th Street, New York 10011

Text copyright © 2009 by Elizabeth Spires
Distributed in Canada by Douglas & McIntyre Ltd.
Printed and bound in China by South China Printing Co. Ltd.
First edition, 2009

The four poems set in italics—"A Vision," "The Gift,"
"A Conversation," and "Wisdom"—are composed of direct quotations from Edmondson,
excerpted from interviews with him in the 1930s and 1940s.

Library of Congress Cataloging-in-Publication Data
Spires, Elizabeth.
    I heard God talking to me : William Edmondson and his stone carvings / Elizabeth Spires.— 1st ed.
        p.   cm.
    ISBN-13: 978-0-374-33528-1
    ISBN-10: 0-374-33528-1
    1. Edmondson, William, 1882?–1951—Poetry.   2. African American artists—Poetry.   3. African
Americans—Poetry.   4. African Americans—Religion—Poetry.   5. Stone carving—Poetry.   I. Title.

PS3569.P554I5 2009
811'.54—dc22

                                                                                2008002343

Designed by Robbin Gourley

www.fsgbooks.com

1   3   5   7   9   10   8   6   4   2

In memory of Louise LeQuire,
generous spirit,
who came to William Edmondson early on

"Pulpit." Tennessee State Museum, Nashville, Tennessee

CONTENTS

William Edmondson's yard.
Untitled, 1941. Photograph by Edward Weston

A VISION

I had a vision.
I was just a boy,
about thirteen, fourteen years old,
doing in the cornfields.
I saw in the east world,
I saw in the west world,
I saw the flood.

I ain't never read no books
nor no Bible,
and I saw the water come.
It come over the rocks,
it covered up the rocks
and went over the mountains.
God, He just showed me how.

William Edmondson with "Noah's Ark." Untitled, 1937. Photograph by Louise Dahl-Wolfe

THE GIFT

One night
God talked so loud He woke me up.
He told me He had something for me.

Later
I was out in the driveway
with some old pieces of stone
when I heard a voice telling me
to pick up my tools
and start to work on a tombstone.
I looked up in the sky
and right there in the noon daylight
He hung a tombstone out for me to make.

I knowed it was God
telling me what to do.
First He told me to make tombstones.
Then He told me to cut the figures.
He gave me them two things.

"William Edmondson, Sculptor, Nashville, 1937." Photograph by Louise Dahl-Wolfe

A CONVERSATION

The Lord told me to cut something once
and I said to myself
I didn't believe I could.
He talked right back to me:
"Yes, you can," He told me.
"Will, cut that stone,
and it better be limestone, too."

So I found some pieces of limestone—
old curbs, sills, steps—
things no one wanted.
And I began to cut on the stone
with an old railroad spike
and a chisel and file.

I'se just doing the Lord's work.
It ain't got much style.
God don't want much style,
but He gives you wisdom
and speeds you along.

"William Edmondson, Primitive Sculptor, Nashville, 1937." Photograph by Louise Dahl-Wolfe

"Seated Girl." Collection of Mr. and Mrs. Jesse M. O. Colton

GIRL THINKING

Once I was a block of stone
in Will Edmondson's yard.
I didn't look like *me* at all.
I waited for what seemed forever,
and then I felt a *tap, tap, tap.*
It was Will Edmondson, taking
a hammer and chisel to me.

> *Make me a girl*, I wished.
> *A girl with a space of quiet around her,*
> *a girl with time to dream her dreams.*
> And he did. He did!

You see, I don't want to grow up,
marry, and have a pack of children.
I don't want to spend my days
cooking, cleaning, and washing clothes.
I want to be who I am now
forever, and I will. I will!
Will Edmondson made sure of that.

"Adam and Eve." The Briskin Family Collection

ADAM AND EVE

There are different kinds of Eden.
Some with high walls and locked gates
where everything is perfect, too perfect,
especially the apple trees.
Would you believe an apple,
one perfect little apple
(with help from *that* serpent),
got us thrown out of Eden?
Does that seem reasonable?
Now, does it?

But here at Will Edmondson's place,
everything grows as it pleases,
and no one is banished
for eating an apple from an apple tree.
There are all sorts here,
preachers and schoolteachers,
shady and upstanding ladies,
and creatures you wouldn't believe,
some humble, some proud,
some quiet, some loud,
everyone just being themselves,
with no voice in the clouds saying,
You can't have an apple,
not one little apple, off my apple tree!

And there in the middle of it all
is Will Edmondson, pleased
with everything he's made
(even that pesky serpent
who follows us everywhere).
It's a different kind of Eden,
arms thrown open to Creation,
and nobody's perfect here,
and nobody tries to be!

"Miss Louisa." Philadelphia Museum of Art

MISS LOUISA

I'm Miss Louisa,
no last name, just Miss Louisa.
I know what you're wondering:
Miss? At your age?
The answer is
No, I never married.

You see this hat I'm holding?
A gentleman asked me
to keep it for him.
Where I come from,
a gentleman's hat is as good
as an engagement ring.

I'm waiting for that gentleman
to come calling again.
Oh, where did he go?
If you see him,
please tell him Miss Louisa
is waiting for him.

"Jack Johnson." The Newark Museum, Newark, N.J. / Art Resource, New York

JACK JOHNSON

What do you know about me?
What do you know?
Do you know I was the world's first
black heavyweight boxing champion?
I defended my title on July 4, 1910,
Independence Day. Now, wasn't that fitting?
I beat Jim Jeffries, a white man,
and that upset a lot of people.

I played bass fiddle.
I liked to read.
When times were tough,
I even acted in vaudeville.

Here's a few more things:
I had gold caps on my teeth, a golden smile.
I believed in a high style of living.
I was a sharp dresser.
I liked diamond stickpins and wide lapels.
I drove fast fancy cars.
Once, I got a $50 ticket for speeding.
When I gave the officer a $100 bill,
he said he didn't have change.
I said, "Keep the change.
I'm coming back the same way I came through."

It was hard being a black man in my time,
but I'm not complaining. I liked to say,
"I was a brunette in a blond town,
but I did not stop steppin'!"

And now that I've had my say,
I have a question for you, Will Edmondson.
Why did you give me all this hair
when you know that I was bald?

"Po'ch Ladies." The Montclair Art Museum, Montclair, N.J.

PORCH LADIES

What's nicer on a hot summer afternoon
than sitting on a big shady porch
swinging on the porch swing?

Our neighborhood's friendly,
not like some places we know.
When someone passes by,
we do what Mama taught us, we call out,
    Good morning, friend!
    Nice day we're having!

Other places are full of rush and bustle,
horns honking and sirens wailing,
radios blaring and buses barreling past,
time rushing everyone along,
too fast, too fast.

But here on the porch
everything moves slow,
slow as molasses,
slow as a seven-year itch,
slow as the day before Christmas.
Slow, we tell you. Slow!

    Hey you, driving that fast car!
    Slow down, for goodness' sake.
    No need to rush so!

So if you hear someone on a porch
call out to you, wave like you mean it,
and hello them right back!
It's the right thing to do.
Mama said so!

"Eleanor Roosevelt." Collection of Catherine King Wieneke

ELEANOR ROOSEVELT

The President and I made a stop in Nashville
on November 17, 1934. Sixteen miles of rope
held back the cheering crowds along the parade route.
We breakfasted at the Hermitage, Andrew Jackson's
home place, then I slipped out back to see the slave quarters
where his faithful servant Uncle Alfred lived out his life.
(Thank goodness times have changed, but if I have my way
they'll change some more, until everyone in this great land
of ours has the same rights and opportunities.
I've told the President how I feel. He doesn't disagree,
but believes the nation must go slow. Why? I wonder. Why?
After all these years of injustice, why must we go slow?)

Do you know what I remember best about that day?
The Jubilee Singers at Fisk, in black-and-white regalia,
singing "Hand Me Down My Silver Trumpet, Gabriel."
Mr. Edmondson, were you in the crowd that day?
I think you were, because you sculpted me
in the overcoat I was wearing, the one with the fur collar.
I'll never forget those thirty golden voices singing
in jubilation, the crowd of five thousand joining in,
Hand me down my silver trumpet, Gabriel!
Hand it down! Throw it down! Any old way to get it down!
That stayed with me as we drove away,
back to our waiting train, headed for Warm Springs, Georgia.

"William Edmondson, Sculptor, Nashville, 1941." Photograph by Edward Weston

SHOES

I've had these shoes as long as I can remember.
Been too preoccupied to get another pair.
On a hot summer day in Nashville
(and all summer days are hot here)
I always say the ven-ti-la-tion's
mighty good in shoes like these.

Sometimes my sister Sarah
calls from the back door,
William, what you doing out there?
The yard needs mowing!
Look at those weeds everywhere!
And when you're finished,
you need to go downtown
and buy yourself a pair of shoes!

But I can't take the time right now,
and spend good money,
when I got work to do.
And breaking in a new pair
is like having a tooth pulled.

Also, if I'm listing reasons,
the spirits in these stones
been waiting a long time
to be what they'll be.
If I went out to buy new shoes,
some poor soul would be waiting
even longer to be free.

So you see, I can't go
to any store right now.
Would you please tell Sarah?

"Rabbit." Collection of Alan W. Zibart

RABBIT

Old Will seen me where I hid . . .

He thunked me with his hammer.
He scraped me with his knife.
He reached in his fingers,
caught hold of my ears,
and drew me right out
of that chunk of limestone!

So here I sit
in Old Will's backyard,
wrinklin' my nose,
smellin' the air,
lookin' this way and that.

It's a funny old place he's got here,
all weeds and tall grass . . .
I think I'll stay awhile.
There over yonder I see two ladies
swinging on a porch swing,
and a girl thinking and thinking and thinking,
and an angel holding tight
to her pocketbook,
and some kind of critter
I can't make heads nor tails of,
and three crows causing a ruckus,
and a talking owl
who's never going to be my friend.

I'll keep away from him!

"Talking Owl." Collection of Estelle E. Friedman

TALKING OWL

I'm silent as a stone all day,
but when the night comes
I roost in the topmost branch of the tree
and look down at the world below,
all marbly white in the moonlight.

The Moon changes everything into a statue.
I see figures here and there in the tall grass,
but I don't know their names
so I say to a rabbit, I say,
Who? Who? Who's there?
But he says, *Keep away, Owl!*
Nobody's here. Nobody!
and skitters away into the tall grass.

Then, lonely, I spread my wings and fly
in widening circles up to the top of the sky
to talk to the old one-eyed Moon,
and I say, *Who? Who?*
Who is the one who made me?
But the Moon just stares and stares,
he won't answer, so my mind widens,
and my *who* grows bigger,
and I fly here, there, everywhere,
until I come to the very edge of the night
where the Stars shine and murmur.

And I say to the Stars, I say,
Who? Who? Who is the one who made me?
And the Stars answer in a tiny whisper
that swirls above, below, and around me:
Will Edmondson made you. That's who!

"Turtle with Young." Collection of Albert Hanover Marlowe

OLD TURTLE

I was a tingle in Old Will's brain,
like lightning getting ready to happen,
then I came out the palm of his hand.

He made my shell a tall round dome.
He made my tail a long stiff bone.
He made my nose just peeping out.
He left my feet tucked all the way inside.

Then Old Will rocked back on his heels,
he rocked and he rocked,
and he said to hisself, he said,
"Something is missing here.
Something is surely missing."

Then he made Young Turtle
and set him on top of my back.
And that tickled him,
it surely did tickle him,
to see a turtle riding piggyback!

"Three Birds." Jill and Sheldon Bonovitz Collection
(The three birds have been variously identified as doves or crows.)

THREE CROWS

We're three crows,
singing a song, crooning a tune,
cawing 'cause we like to.

We're hipsters,
we're bebop birds,
we jive and we groove,

'cause Will made us
cooler than cool, three crows
looking over your shoulder,

jazzed up, ready to roll,
though some say
we're songsters who can't sing,

flat, off-key,
out of sync with everything,
but who you gonna believe, us or them?

"Critter." Cheekwood Museum of Art, Nashville, Tennessee

NIECES AND NEPHEWS

Uncle Will was always carving,
carving them stones.
But he liked to have fun, too.

One day he made a game out of it.
Tap, tap, tap . . .
That old block of limestone
began to look like nothing
we'd ever seen before.
We didn't think he was finished
when he put down his tools
and washed the dust off his hands.

And we said,
"Uncle Will, you ain't done
with that one yet!"

But he nodded he was,
and began to chuckle.

So we started pestering him . . .
Was it a buffalo?
An ox?
A horse?
A mule?

"You ain't close," he said.
"You ain't even close.
It's a critter,
just a critter.
Ain't you ever seen a critter before?"

And he laughed so hard
he doubled up.

"Birdbath." Present owner unknown

BIRDBATH

Could you do what I do?
Could you balance this birdbath
on top of your head day and night?
Spring and fall?
Summer and winter?
Could you?

And never get tired or sleepy?
And never tip over?
And never say, *Enough! I quit!*
(Quitting is not an option.)

I have a lot of time to think.
A lot of time to watch
the sun rise each morning,
to listen to a chattering in the trees
that grows louder and louder and louder
as I say to myself, I say,
Let the birds come.
I'm ready!

"Mermaid." Collection of Gael and Michael Mendelsohn

MERMAID

Some hearts are light as a feather,
and some are heavy as stone.
If you think my heart is heavy,
you'd be wrong, you'd be wrong.

Some people go through life
doubting who they are,
or what they want to be.
But not me, not me!

Words are a funny thing:
inside each *impossibility*
is *possibility*. And inside *stone*
you may find *one* like me.

I can still hear Will Edmondson
chuckling when he made me—
a stone mermaid who lives
a thousand miles from the sea.

Some hearts are light as a feather,
and some are heavy as stone.
If you think my heart is heavy,
well, you're wrong, you're wrong!

William Edmondson's hands. Untitled, 1937. Photograph by Louise Dahl-Wolfe

HANDS

These hands have raked and plowed and planted.
These hands have swept and scrubbed.
These hands have pushed brooms, mended shoes,
brushed the back of a horse until it glistened.
Oh, these hands have done so many things!

These hands have worked all day,
every day, doing what the Lord wants.
These hands are older now, covered in dust.
Sometimes they're stiff in the morning,
but these hands have more to do.

These hands were made by His hand,
and won't stop, can't stop,
not yet, not now,
until *He* tells me they can.

"Williams Tombstone." Tennessee State Museum, Nashville, Tennessee

A TOMBSTONE TALKS

There's no good time to die,
that's for certain, but I was young,
too young, when I passed on.
It was during the Great Depression.

My family asked Will Edmondson
to carve me a plain stone,
but when the time came to pay,
they didn't have the money.

Most likely, he would have let them
have it anyway, but they didn't ask.
Why? I wonder. Why?
Oh, what can you do with a tombstone
once somebody's name is attached?

So now I lie in an unmarked grave,
anonymous as a blade of grass.
But I won't be forgotten.
Because of Will Edmondson,
my name lives on in a museum:

    BERNICE WILLIAMS

"Angel with a Pocketbook." Collection of Estelle E. Friedman

ANGEL WITH A POCKETBOOK

I never thought I'd get to heaven, but I did.
I closed my eyes and died, then flew straight up
through clouds that looked like cotton candy,
clutching my pocketbook. The angel at the gate
said I wouldn't need a pocketbook in heaven,
but I held on tight and said I would.
We argued for a while and then he let me in.
Which proves that stubbornness must be a virtue.
At least sometimes.

As you can see, I'm not the airy, wings-aflutter sort.
I'm a two-feet-on-the-ground, no-nonsense type
who can't carry a tune for trying, and heights,
even a choir loft, make me dizzy.
But Heaven, I'm told, is interested in goodness,
not sameness, and though it's not for me
to judge how good I was in life,
somebody must have thought I was,
or else why would I be here?

Of course, I'd rather be in heaven
than you-know-where, but I'll confess
sometimes I miss how *real* the earth was,
miss lipstick, hairdos, the sound of my high heels
click-click-clicking on the sidewalk,
pocketbook swinging at my side.

It's foggy here and every time I take a step
I sink a little into cloud, then bounce back up.
They say, just give it time and my memories
will fade like a dress left hanging in the sun.
That soon I'll throw a choir robe over my head
and, with a *Hallelujah!*, sing as good as anyone.
Until that happens, I'm keeping my pocketbook!

"William Edmondson, Sculptor, Nashville, 1937." Photograph by Louise Dahl-Wolfe

ICE

It's funny what a body will remember.
I remember Nashville's great ice storm
on January 31, 1951.
Oh, it was cold. Cold!
The cold seeped like smoke through
every crack and cranny in the house.

I was upstairs in bed,
the quilts piled on.
Could hardly trouble myself
to get out of bed or eat a thing,
I felt that poorly.
But when the sun rose that morning,
I saw a sight that lifted my heart
straight up to the ceiling.

    All the trees in the orchard,
    every last twig and branch,
    were coated with ice, glittering ice,
    shining like diamonds in the sun.

Oh, the Lord keeps surprises up his sleeve.
No doubt about that!
(He had one in store for me, too.)

For a week, whenever the wind blew,
there was a sound like breaking glass.
Then the rains came,
and all that glittering ice just melted away.
The next day, February 7, I died.
Don't act surprised.
Dying, like living, has to happen.

"Tombstones." Photograph by Roger Haile

ARARAT

Mt. Ararat Cemetery, Nashville

I died and went to Ararat.
It's quiet here.
A little overgrown.
Reminds me of back home.

The soul's a bird
that rests here for a while,
then flies off, disappears.
I died and went to Ararat.

I'm here but not here.
My tombstone's gone,
my grave is overgrown.
I died and went to Ararat.

My spirit's in the stones
of all the people here.
I died and went to Ararat.
I'm here. I'm home.

"William Edmondson, Tennessee, 1941." Photograph by Edward Weston

WISDOM

Wisdom,
that's what the Lord
gave me at birth,
but I didn't know it
till He came and told me about it.
It's wonderful when God
gives you something.
You've got it for good,
and yet you ain't got it.
You got to do it and work for it.

I do according to the wisdom of God.
He gives me mind and hand,
and then I go ahead and carve
these things you see here.

William Edmondson's yard. Untitled, 1941. Photograph by Edward Weston

ABOUT
WILLIAM
EDMONDSON

William Edmondson, the second child of freed slaves Orange Edmondson and Jane Brown Edmondson, was born in December 1874 on a former plantation outside Nashville, Tennessee. Record-keeping was casual in those days, and the exact date of his birth, recorded in the family Bible, was destroyed by fire. In later years, when asked his age, Edmondson would simply say, "How old I is got burnt up."

Edmondson never attended school or learned to read and write. His early years were spent working as a hired hand for Henry W. Compton, a white landowner, on the land where he was born. His wages as a field hand would probably have been somewhere around ten or twelve dollars a month. Looking back at those hard times, Edmondson would later say, "God didn't intend anyone to work themselves to death. Slave time is over."

When Edmondson was sixteen, he found work in Nashville, a three-mile walk from the Compton plantation. Over time, all five of his brothers and sisters—Ellen, Sara, Richard, Orange Jr., and James—also found jobs in Nashville, and moved there with their mother, leaving the Compton plantation for good. Edmondson held various jobs, working in the city sewer works and as a racehorse swipe, before being hired by the Nashville, Chattanooga & St. Louis Railway. In 1907, he injured his leg and lost his job. After that, he worked for almost twenty-five years as a janitor and orderly at the Women's Hospital in Nashville until it closed in 1931.

Edmondson had, since he was a boy, experienced religious visions in which he heard and saw God speaking to him. His memory of his first vision was vivid: "I was just a little boy about thirteen, fourteen years old, doing in the cornfields. I saw in the east world, I saw in the west world, I saw the flood. I ain't never read no books nor no Bible, and I saw the water come. It come over the rocks, covered up the rocks, and went over the mountains. God, He just showed me how."

More visions followed in Edmondson's middle and later years. One in particular called him toward the vocation of stonecutting: "I was out in the driveway with some old pieces of stone when I heard a voice telling me to pick up my tools and start to work on a tombstone. I looked up in the sky and right there in the noon daylight He hung a tombstone out for me to make . . . I knowed it was God telling me what to do. God was telling me to cut figures. First He told me to make tombstones. Then He told me to cut the figures. He gave me them two things."

So, around the age of fifty-seven, Edmondson began carving stone. For two years, he concentrated on tombstones. Self-taught, if divinely inspired, he used the tools at hand: a railroad spike (later, a chisel), a short-handled hammer, and a file. Gradually, as he became more confident of his abilities, he began carving garden ornaments, whimsical birdbaths, animals, and, most important, stylized human figures that had great presence and individuality.

Edmondson liked to say that he carved "stingily." Economical by necessity, he used small, irregular pieces of limestone that he could buy cheaply from a nearby quarry or scavenge for free from demolished buildings, streets, and sidewalks. Sometimes friends and neighbors brought him stone. The dimensions of the irregular stone pieces he used dictated the small, compact size of his figures.

His studio was a long three-sided shed, one end open to the weather, next to his house at 1434 Fourteenth Avenue South in Nashville. He worked in full view of his family, including nieces and nephews, the neighbors, and passersby. In cold weather, he carved next to a coal stove to keep warm. As new sculptures were finished, they joined a lively congregation in his yard.

He hung out a hand-lettered sign to attract customers:

TOMB-STONES.
FOR SALE.
GARDEN. ORNAMENTS.
STONE WORK Wm EDMONDSON.

In a time when Nashville's neighborhoods, schools, churches, and cemeteries were racially segregated, Edmondson's first customers would have been black families in need of simple, inexpensive tombstones. As word spread of his talents, people from more distant, well-off white neighborhoods came to buy his animal and human figures.

Sidney Hirsch, a faculty member at George Peabody College for Teachers, often passed by Edmondson's yard. A poet and a mystic, Hirsch collected art and cultural artifacts from around the world. One day, intrigued by Edmondson's sculptures, he struck up a conversation. As the two got to know each other, Hirsch took many of his friends to see Edmondson's work, including Alfred and Elizabeth Starr, who began buying pieces from Edmondson. The Starrs introduced Edmondson to Louise Dahl-Wolfe, a photographer from New York City who worked for the fashion magazine *Harper's Bazaar.*

Dahl-Wolfe, intrigued by Edmondson's sculptures, took over a hundred photographs of Edmondson and his work. Returning to New York, she showed them to her friend Thomas Mabry, a curator at the Museum of Modern Art. He and Alfred Barr, the director of the museum, arranged for an exhibit at MoMA of twelve of Edmondson's sculptures, which ran from October 20 to December 1, 1937, making Edmondson the first black artist to have a solo show at that prestigious institution.

The next year, Edmondson's work was included in the exhibit "Three Centuries of Art in the United States" at the Musée du Jeu de Paume in Paris, France. But despite the attention he received in New York and Paris, it was not until 1941 that his work was publicly displayed in Nashville, at the Nashville Art Gallery on Union Street. That same year, the well-known photographer Edward Weston also visited Edmondson and took photographs. Although his work had received favorable attention in New York, with reviews in *The New York Times,* *Newsweek,* and *Time,* in Nashville Edmondson's sculptures sold for modest prices, sometimes for as little as five or ten dollars. As he explained to John Thompson, a reporter at the local newspaper *The Nashville Tennessean,* "I got to do these things for my Heavenly Daddy, whether folks buys them or not. He ain't never said nothin' 'bout pay for it."

Although Edmondson often carved ordinary people—schoolteachers, preachers, and "little ladies," as he called them—he also had his heroines and heroes. First Lady Eleanor Roosevelt, who championed the dignity and equality of all people, regardless of race, was one, carved by Edmondson after her 1934 visit to Nashville with President Roosevelt. The black prizefighters Jack Johnson and Joe Louis were two others, who both won world heavyweight boxing titles, in 1908 and 1937, respectively. And, of course, Edmondson took inspiration from the Bible, carving many angels and crucifixes, as well as Adam and Eve, Mary and Martha, and Noah's Ark.

Edmondson continued to carve until 1948, when poor health forced him to stop. All told, he probably carved over three hundred sculptures in the seventeen-year period between 1931 and 1948. He died on February 7, 1951, and was buried in Nashville's oldest black cemetery, Mt. Ararat (now Greenwood Cemetery West). His gravestone, like many others there, has long since disappeared, and the records that would tell where he was buried no longer exist. Obituaries appeared in newspapers and magazines across the country, including *The New York Times, Art Digest, The Nashville Tennessean,* and *The Nashville Banner.* After his death, his relatives, apparently unaware of the extent of Edmondson's reputation, sold the remaining carvings out of his yard for as little as twenty dollars each.

Edmondson's house and studio no longer stand, torn down to make way for the Murrell School. In June 1979, a small strip of land at Seventeenth North Avenue and Charlotte Avenue, near downtown Nashville, was designated William Edmondson Park. Except for a mural, it remains undeveloped. In 1981, the Tennessee State Museum's inaugural exhibit was a retrospective of Edmondson's work. Other exhibits followed, most notably a large-scale retrospective of fifty-seven Edmondson sculptures, organized by the Cheekwood Museum of Art in Nashville in 2000–01.

Since his death, the quiet interest in William Edmondson's work has slowly grown, sustained by his many admirers and collectors. His sculptures are now part of the permanent collections of many museums, including the American Folk Art Museum in New York City; the National Museum of American Art and the Hirshhorn Museum in Washington, D.C.; the Philadelphia Museum of Art; the Abby Aldrich Rockefeller Art Center in Williamsburg, Virginia; and the Montclair Museum in New Jersey. The Cheekwood Museum of Art in Nashville, with twenty-one Edmondson sculptures, eleven of which are on permanent display, has the largest collection of his work in the country. The Newark Museum in New Jersey has the next largest with nineteen, and the Tennessee State Museum in Nashville has six. And just a few miles from where Edmondson was born, six of his modest, hand-lettered tombstones still stand in a small hillside cemetery outside Nashville.

If Edmondson were alive today, he probably would be surprised to see his sculptures selling for as much as $300,000. As he once told Nashville reporter John Thompson, "I'se just doin' the Lord's Work. I didn't know I was no artist till them folks told me I was."

A fellow Nashville sculptor, Puryear Mims (1906–1975), who knew and admired Edmondson and his work, paid him this tribute: "The Lord told him to praise His name in stone. With a few crude tools and a myriad forest of grave-stones he sought his way toward his meaningful world. He looked upon stone and the stone looked upon him and he doubled in memory the instinct of a sculptor . . . Today he is part of our world. His images are omnipresent. They tease us out of heart. They say to us, as they did to Will Edmondson, 'I am locked in a stone. I am locked in a heart. Let me out—let me out.'"

SELECTED BIBLIOGRAPHY

The Art of William Edmondson. Nashville: Cheekwood Museum of Art and University Press of Mississippi, 1999.

Fletcher, Georgeanne, and Jym Knight. *William Edmondson: A Retrospective.* Nashville: Tennessee Arts Commission, 1981.

Freeman, Rusty. "William Edmondson at Cheekwood." *Folk Art,* Spring 2000: 30–37.

Fuller, Edmund L. *Visions in Stone: The Sculpture of William Edmondson.* Pittsburgh: The University of Pittsburgh Press, 1973.

"Inspired, Self-Taught Artist, William Edmondson, Dies." *The Nashville Tennessean,* February 9, 1951: 1, 6.

LeQuire, Louise. "Edmondson's Art Reflects His Faith, Strong and Pure." *Smithsonian Magazine,* August 1981: 51–55.

Lindsey, Jack. *Miracles: The Sculptures of William Edmondson.* Philadelphia: Janet Fleisher Gallery, 1994.

"Mirkels." *Time,* November 1, 1937: 52.

"Modern Art Museum and Simple Faith Bring Fame to Sculptor." *Newsweek,* October 25, 1937: 22.

"Modern Museum to Show Negro Art." *The New York Times,* October 9, 1937: 21.

"Negro Who Turned Sculptor at God's Command Gets Manhattan Exhibition." *Life,* November 1, 1937: 79.

Thompson, John. "Negro Stone Cutter Here Says Gift from Lord; Work Praised." *The Nashville Tennessean,* February 9, 1941: 11A.

Wibking, Angela. "Carving a Name." *Nashville Scene,* January 31, 2000.

"William Edmondson, a Primitive Sculptor." *The New York Times,* February 10, 1951: 13.

"William Edmondson Dies." *Art Digest,* March 1, 1951: 13.

Woolsey, F. W. "Edmondson's Visions in Stone." *Look,* October 21, 1952: 61–63.

PHOTO CREDITS
AND ACKNOWLEDGMENTS

Grateful acknowledgment is made to the following museums, private collectors, and photographers for permission to reproduce the images in this book.

Jacket: "William Edmondson, Sculptor, Nashville, Tennessee, 1937": Photograph by Louise Dahl-Wolfe. Collection: Center for Creative Photography, University of Arizona. Copyright © 1989 Arizona Board of Regents.

Facing contents page: "Pulpit" (25½ x 36¼ x 9½). The Tennessee State Museum, Nashville, Tenn. Photograph by Louise LeQuire.

p.1: Untitled, 1941. Photograph by Edward Weston. Collection: Center for Creative Photography, University of Arizona. Copyright © 1989 Arizona Board of Regents.

p. 3: Untitled, 1937. Photograph by Louise Dahl-Wolfe. Collection: Center for Creative Photography, University of Arizona. Copyright © 1989 Arizona Board of Regents.

p. 5: "William Edmondson, Sculptor, Nashville, 1937." Photograph by Louise Dahl-Wolfe. Collection: Center for Creative Photography, University of Arizona. Copyright © 1989 Arizona Board of Regents.

p. 7: "William Edmondson, Primitive Sculptor, Nashville, 1937." Photograph by Louise Dahl-Wolfe. Collection: Center for Creative Photography, University of Arizona. Copyright © 1989 Arizona Board of Regents.

p. 8: "Seated Girl" (21 x 7 x 10½ inches). Collection of Mr. and Mrs. Jesse M. O. Colton. Photograph by Armen.

p. 10: "Adam and Eve" (13 x 30 x 12 inches). The Briskin Family Collection. Photograph by Frank Maresca.

p. 12: "Miss Louisa" (20½ x 6 x 7½ inches). Philadelphia Museum of Art: Gift of Paul W. McCloskey in memory of Maris Madeira McCloskey, 1995. Photograph by Graydon Wood.

p. 14: "Jack Johnson" (16½ x 8 x 8 inches). The Newark Museum, Newark, N.J. / Art Resource, New York.

p. 16: "Po'ch Ladies" (11¾ x 13½ x 15½ inches). Collection of the Montclair Art Museum, Montclair, N.J. Museum purchase; funds provided by the William Lightfoot Schultz Foundation, 1973.2.

p. 18: "Eleanor Roosevelt" (20 x 13 x 6½ inches). Collection of Catherine King Wieneke. Photograph by Louise LeQuire.

p. 20: "William Edmondson, Sculptor, Nashville, 1941." Photograph by Edward Weston. Collection: Center for Creative Photography, University of Arizona. Copyright © 1989 Arizona Board of Regents.

p. 22: "Rabbit" (14¾ x 4¼ x 8¼ inches). Collection of Alan W. Zibart. Photograph by Rusty Freeman.

p. 24: "Talking Owl" (22½ x 18 x 7½ inches). Collection of Estelle E. Friedman. Photograph by Edward Owen.

p. 26: "Turtle with Young" (8½ x 20 x 10¼ inches). Collection of Albert Hanover Marlowe. Photograph by Roger Haile.

p. 28: "Three Birds" (7¼ x 10 x 6 inches). Jill and Sheldon Bonovitz Collection. Photograph courtesy of Fleisher Ollman Gallery.

p. 30: "Critter" (19⅜ x 5⅛ x 22½ inches). Collection of Cheekwood Museum of Art, Nashville, Tenn. Photograph and copyright: Harry Butler, Nashville. Used by permission.

p. 32: "Birdbath" (39⅞ x 21¾ x 17 inches). Present owner unknown. Photograph by Louise LeQuire.

p. 34: "Mermaid" (13½ x 32 x 6 inches). Collection of Gael and Michael Mendelsohn. Photograph by Fred Giampietro.

p. 36: Untitled, 1937. Photograph by Louise Dahl-Wolfe. Collection: Center for Creative Photography, University of Arizona. Copyright © 1989 Arizona Board of Regents.

p. 38: "Williams Tombstone" (17¼ x 11¾ x 5½ inches). The Tennessee State Museum, Nashville, Tenn. Photograph by Louise LeQuire.

p. 40: "Angel with a Pocketbook" (23 x 12½ x 6½ inches). Collection of Estelle E. Friedman. Photograph by Michael Hall.

p. 42: "William Edmondson, Sculptor, Nashville, 1937." Photograph by Louise Dahl-Wolfe. Collection: Center for Creative Photography, University of Arizona. Copyright © 1989 Arizona Board of Regents.

p. 44: "Tombstones." Photograph by Roger Haile. The tombstones are in the cemetery of the Greater Pleasant View Missionary Baptist Church, Brentwood, Tennessee.

p. 46: "William Edmondson, Tennessee, 1941." Photograph by Edward Weston. Collection: Center for Creative Photography, University of Arizona. Copyright © 1989 Arizona Board of Regents.

p. 48: Untitled, 1941. Photograph by Edward Weston. Collection: Center for Creative Photography, University of Arizona. Copyright © 1989 Arizona Board of Regents.